My First Hindi Words!

By Reena Bhansali

For Kaya, Rohnav & Dhara

Seb

SAYB

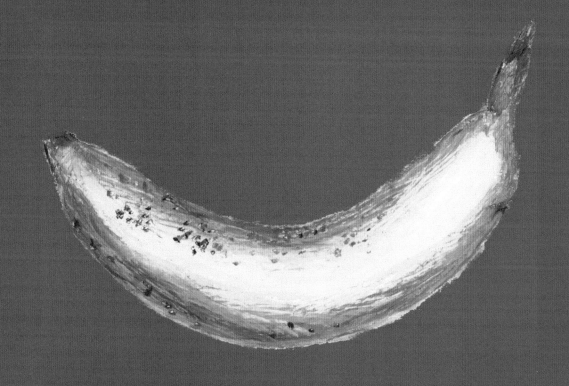

kela

KAY-LAH

Pani
PAH-NEE

Doodh

DUDE

Khaana

KHAA-NAH

Joota
JOO-TAH

KapRe

KUP-RAY

Chashme

CHAH-SH-MAY

Topi
TOH-PEE

Ghar

GHUH-R

kursi

KUR-SEE

Darvaaza

DAR-VAH-ZAH

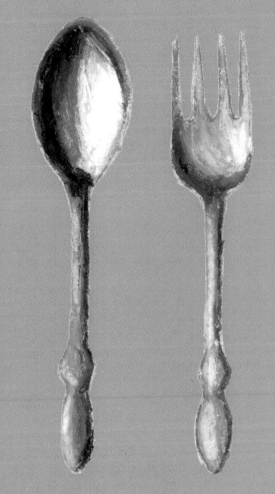

Chamach & Kaanta

CHAH-MUCH & KAA*-TAH

*nasal sound

katori

KUH-TOH-REE

Bistar

BIS-TAHR

Kitaab

KI-TAAB

Saabun

SAA-BOON

Dabba

DUH-BAH

Kutta

KOO-TAH

Billi
BILLY

Haathi
HAA-THEE

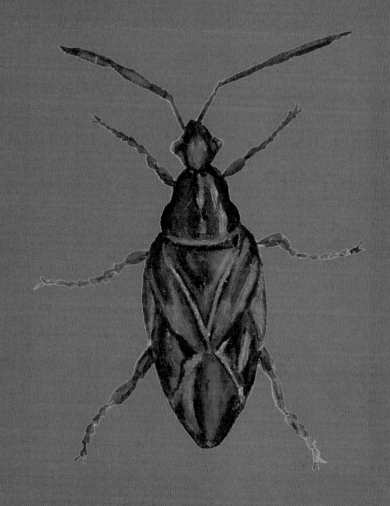

KeeRa

KEE-RAH

phool

PHOO-L

GaaRi

GAA-REE

Check Out Our Other Hindi Books

"My First Hindi Words! Things That Go!"

"My First Hindi Words! Opposites"

Available on www.HindiByReena.com & Amazon.

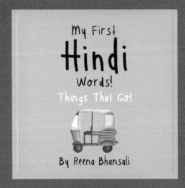

About the Author

Reena Bhansali is the author and illustrator of the "My First Hindi Words!" books. She also owns Hindi By Reena, a one-stop-shop for Hindi kids books, courses, learning tips and products. She grew up in New Delhi and the US.

Printed in Great Britain
by Amazon